A TRIP TO THE DOCTOR

BY MARGOT LINN
PICTURES BY CATHERINE SIRACUSA

HARPER & ROW, PUBLISHERS

Where is Joey going?
To the doctor's examining room.
What will he sit on?
See if you can guess.

tree stump

elephant

table

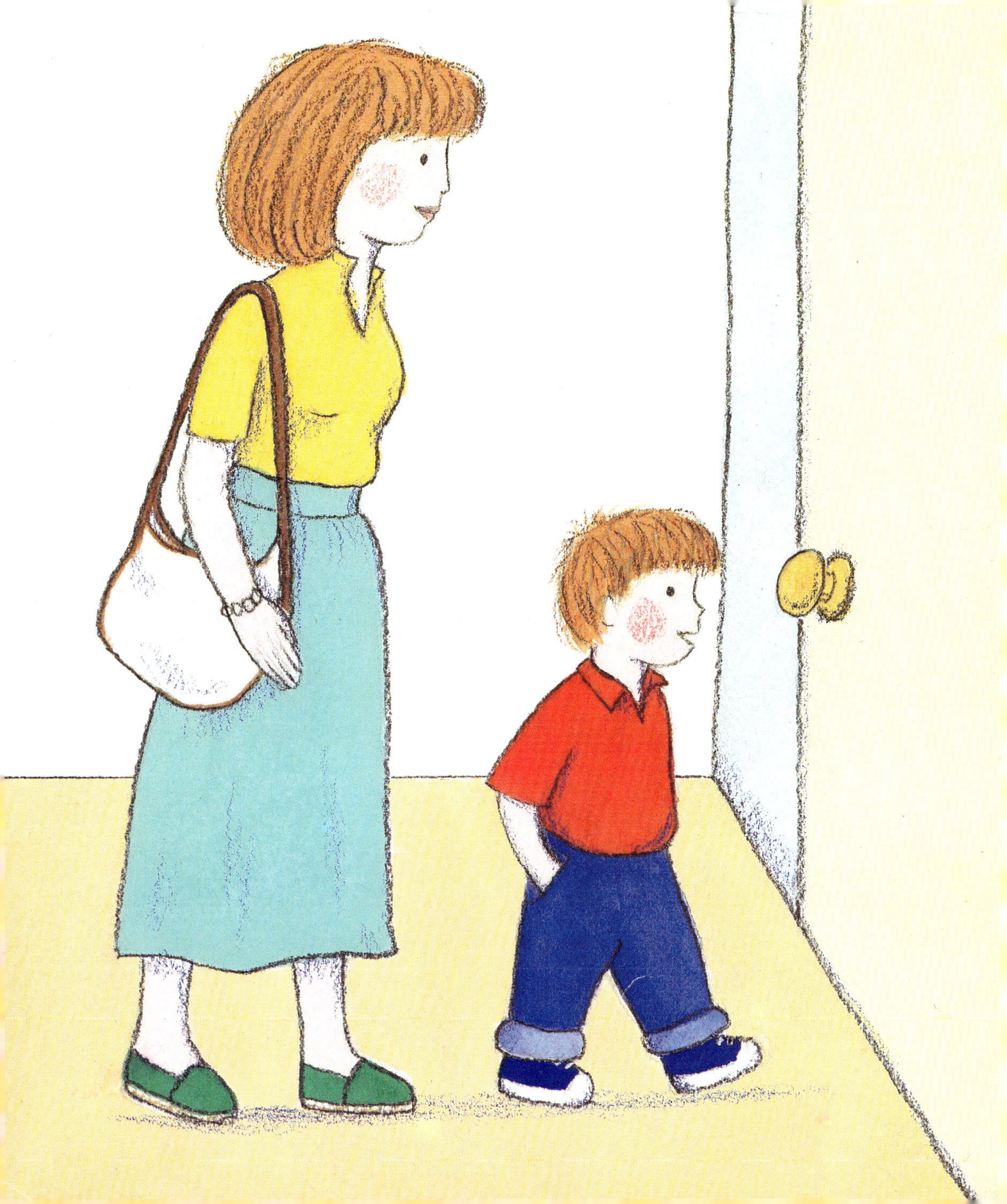

has crinkly, clean paper on it.

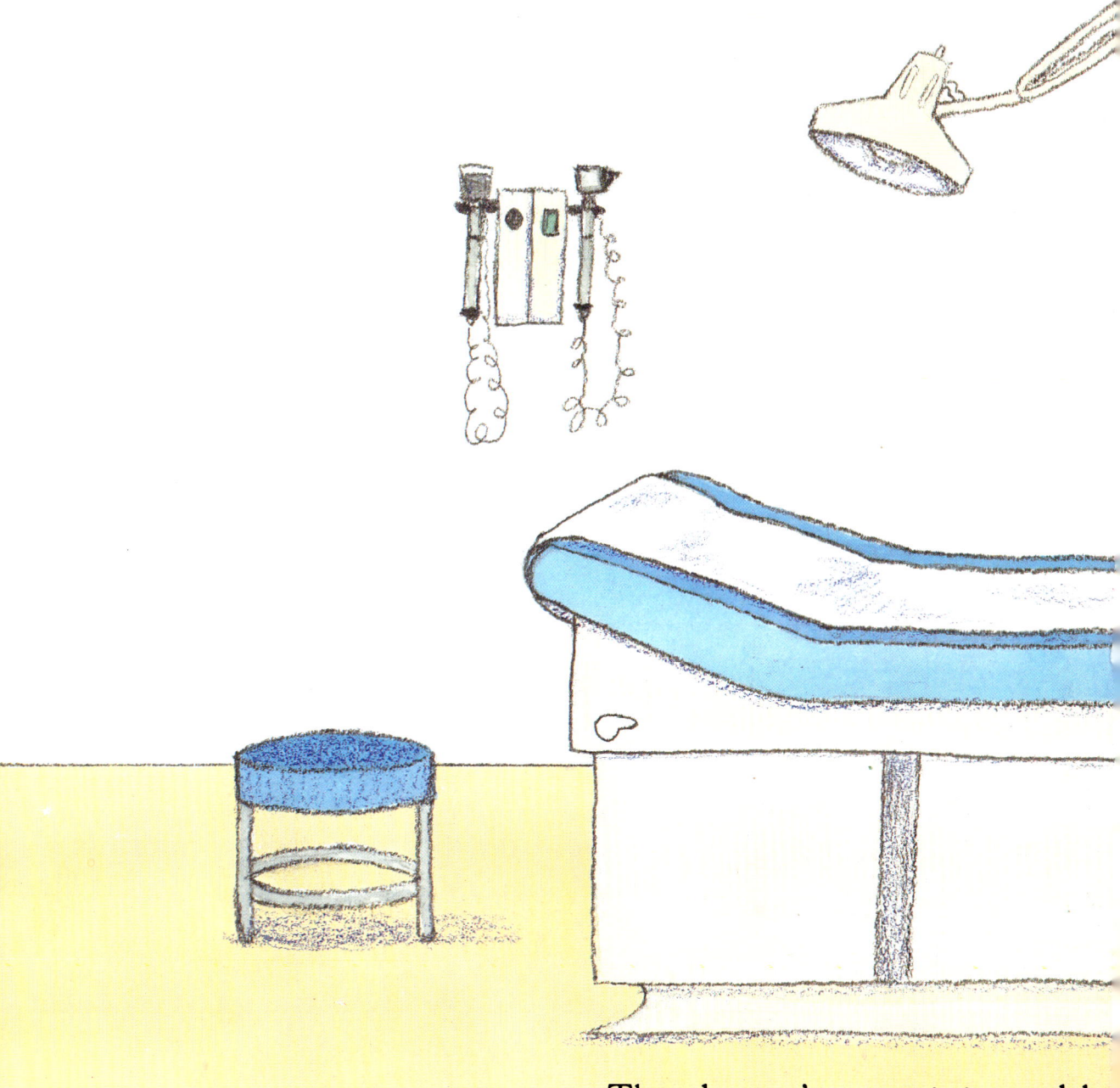

The doctor's examining table

Who is going to weigh and measure Joey?
The nurse.
What will Joey stand on?
See if you can guess.

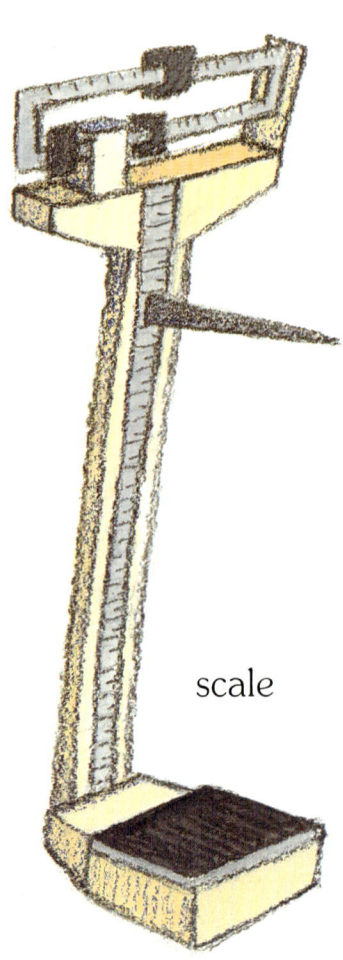

stool

skateboard

scale

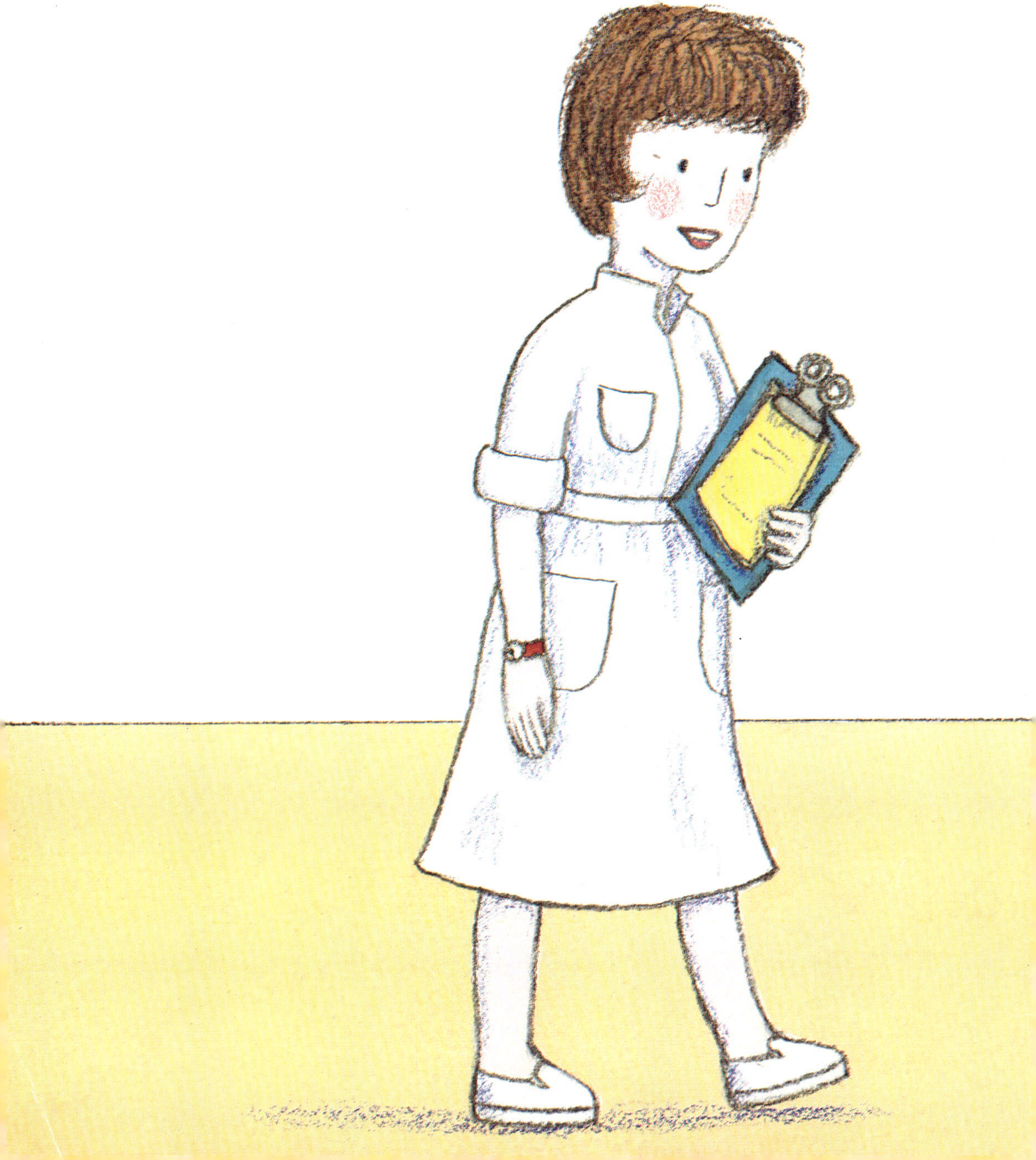

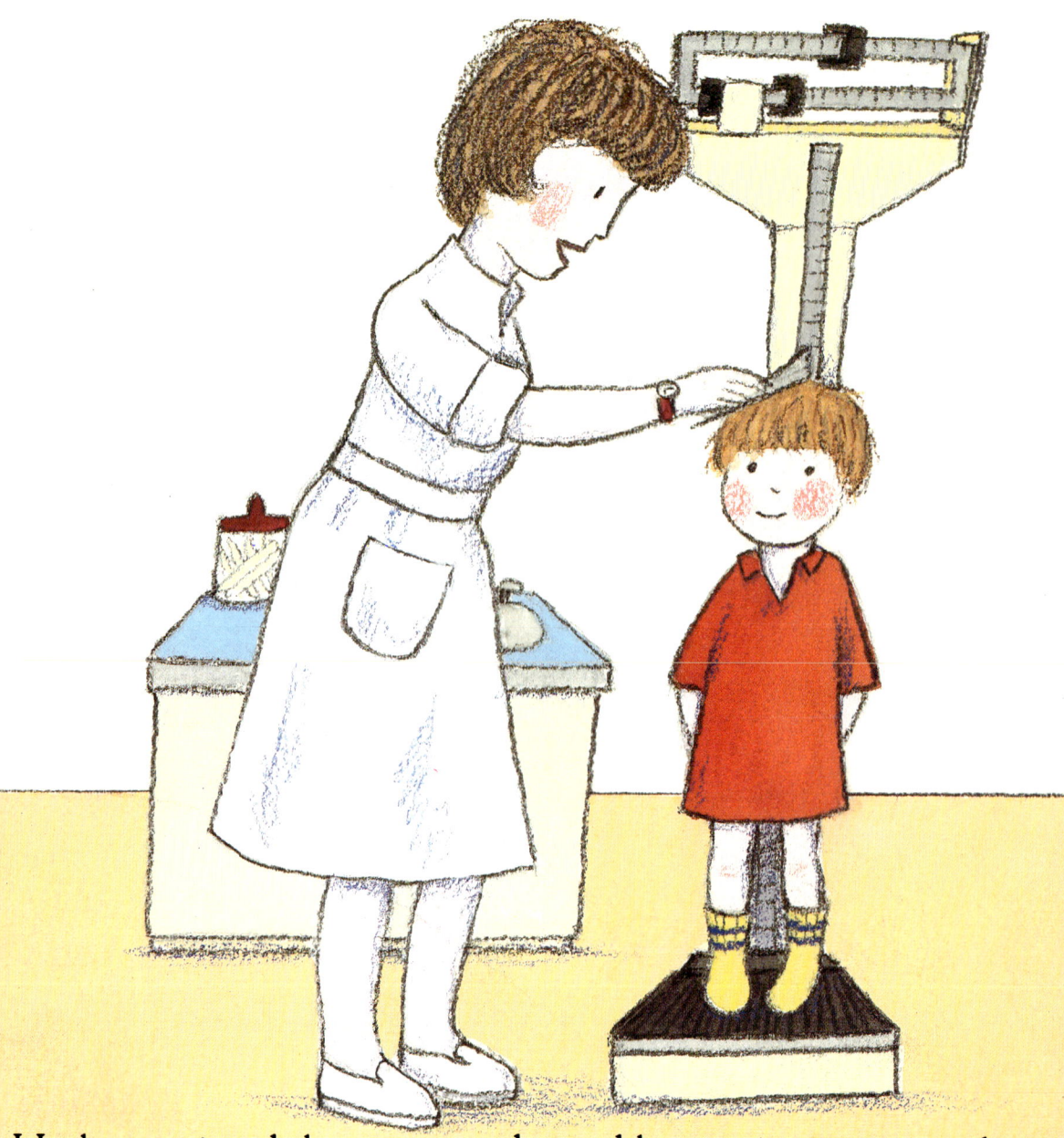

He has gained three pounds and has grown one inch.

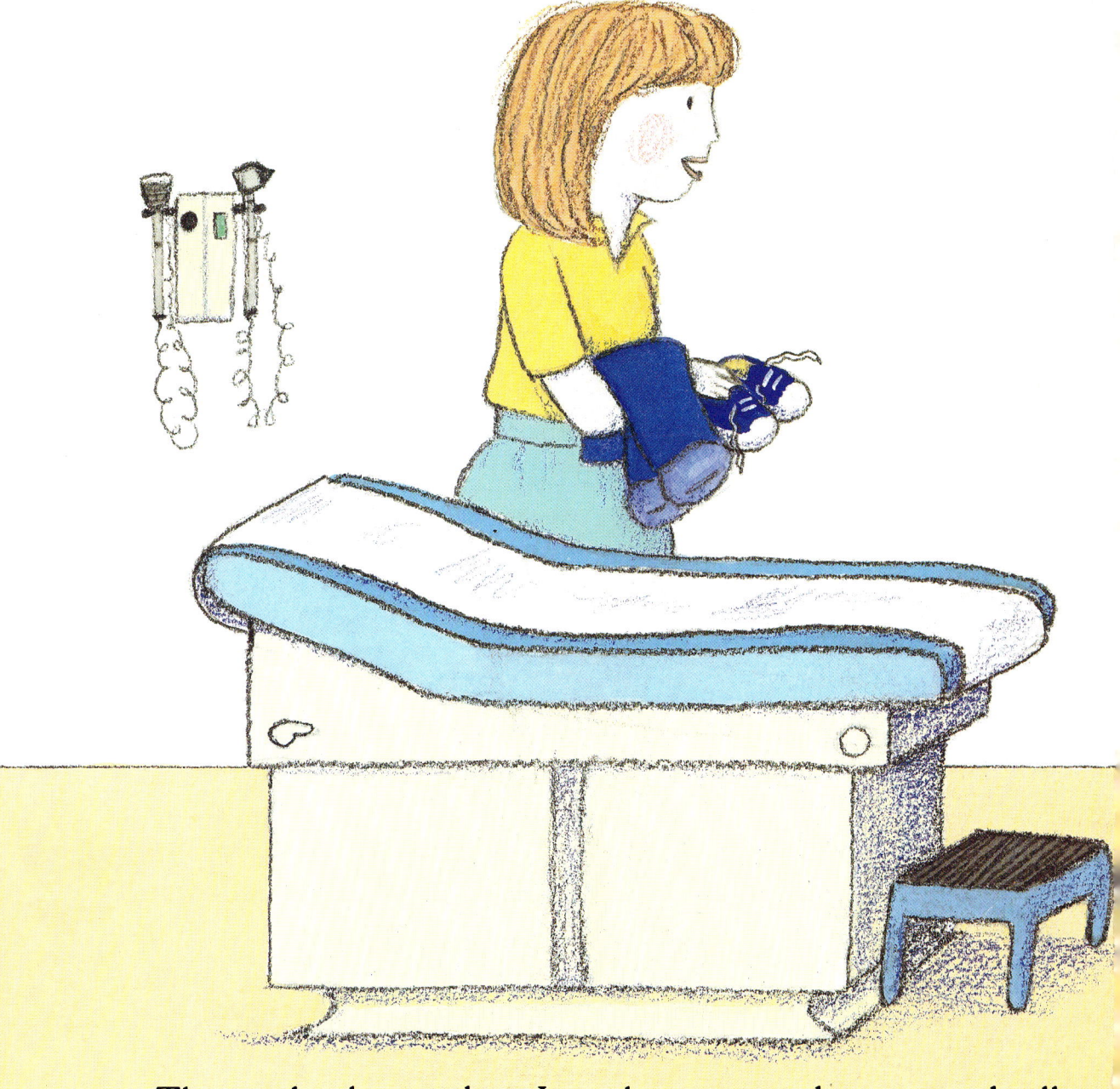

The scale shows that Joey has grown bigger and taller.

Who is going to check Joey's ears?
The doctor.
What will he use?
See if you can guess.

otoscope

earmuffs

horn

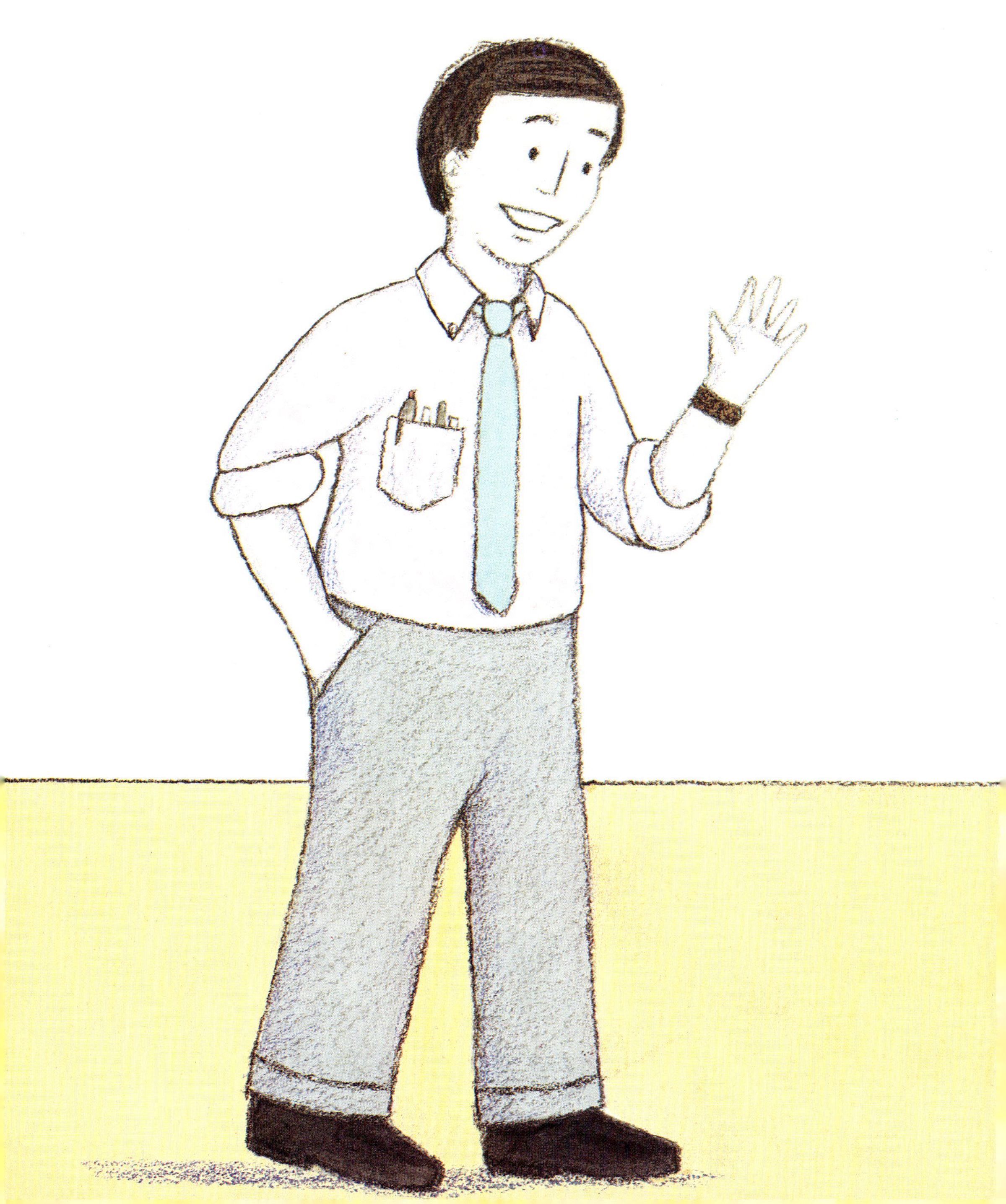

into his ears with an otoscope.

Joey sits still while the doctor looks

Who is going to check Joey's mouth and throat?
The doctor.
What will he use?
See if you can guess.

teddy bear

ice-cream cone

tongue depressor

light

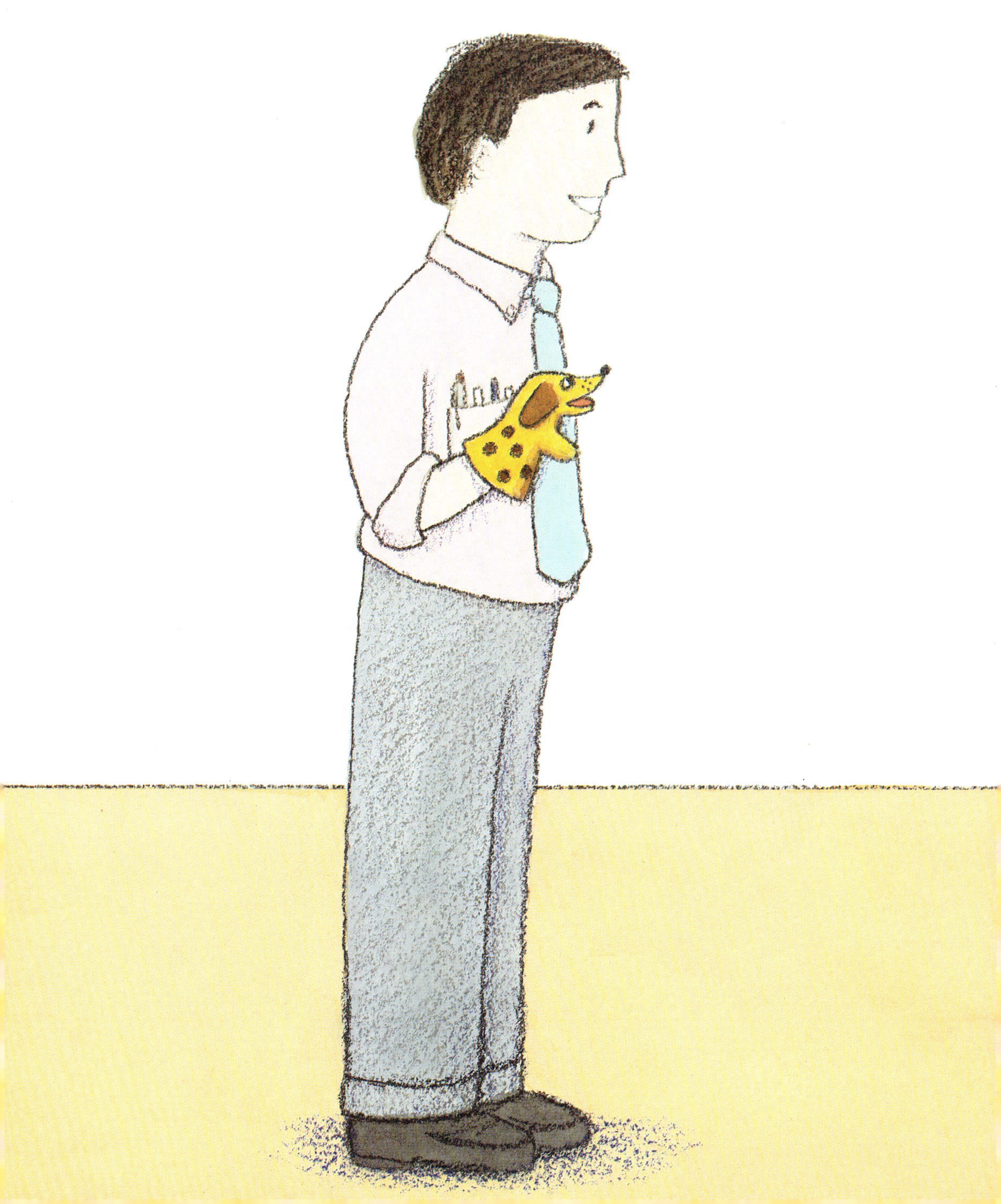

the doctor can see
healthy pink.

With a light and a tongue depressor
that Joey's mouth and throat are a

Who is going to listen to Joey's heart and lungs?
The doctor—and Joey, too!
What will they use?
See if you can guess.

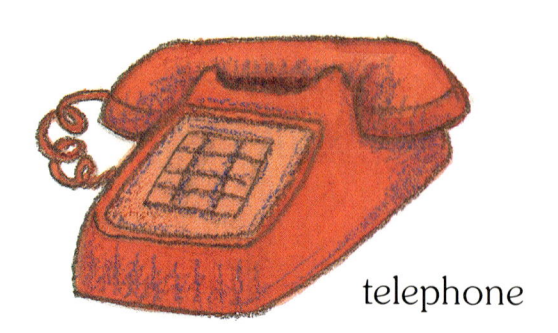

telephone

cake

stethoscope

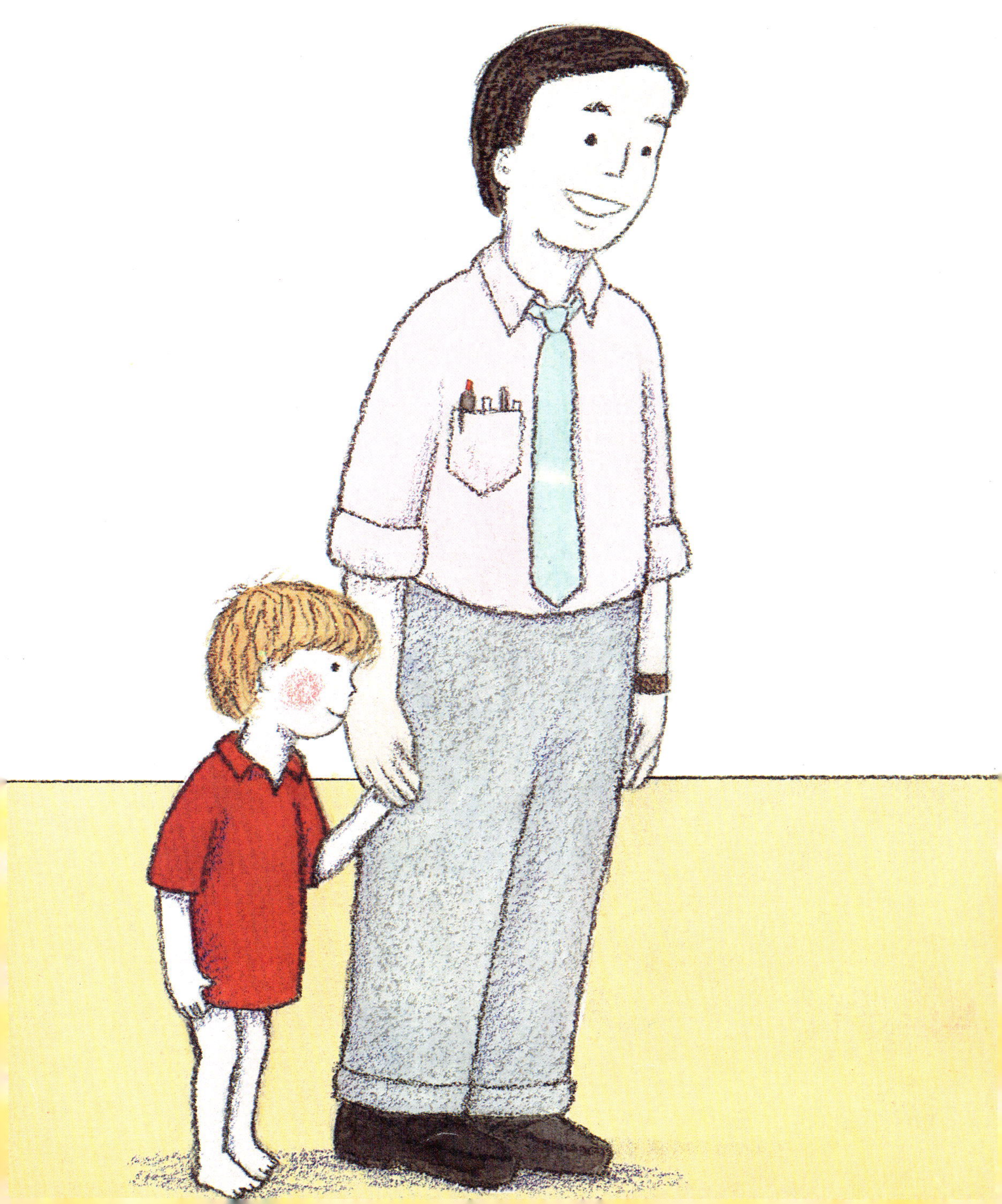

through his stethoscope.
thump-thump, **thump**-thump.

The doctor can hear Joey's heart
It sounds like this: **thump**-thump,

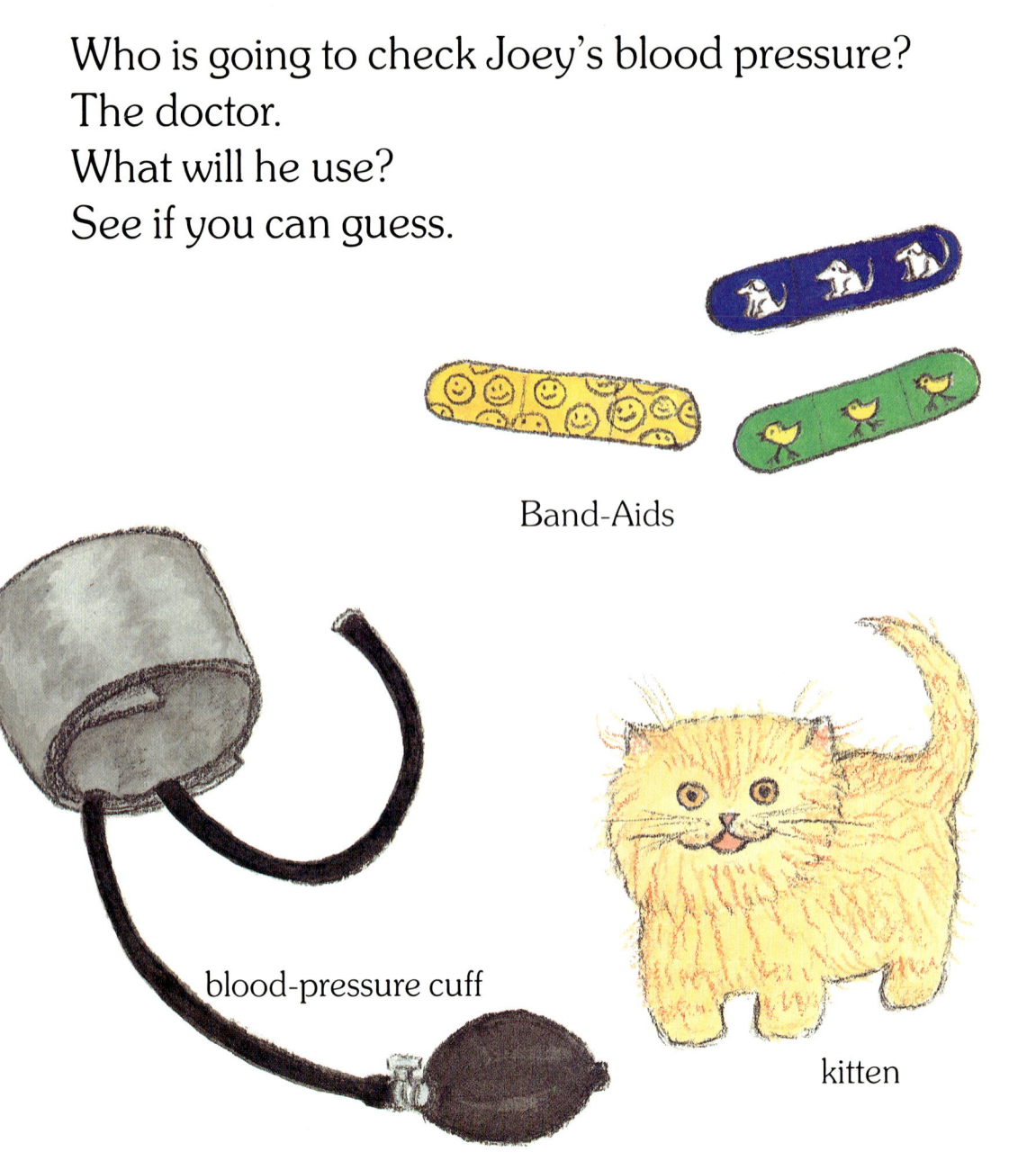

Who is going to check Joey's blood pressure?
The doctor.
What will he use?
See if you can guess.

Band-Aids

blood-pressure cuff

kitten

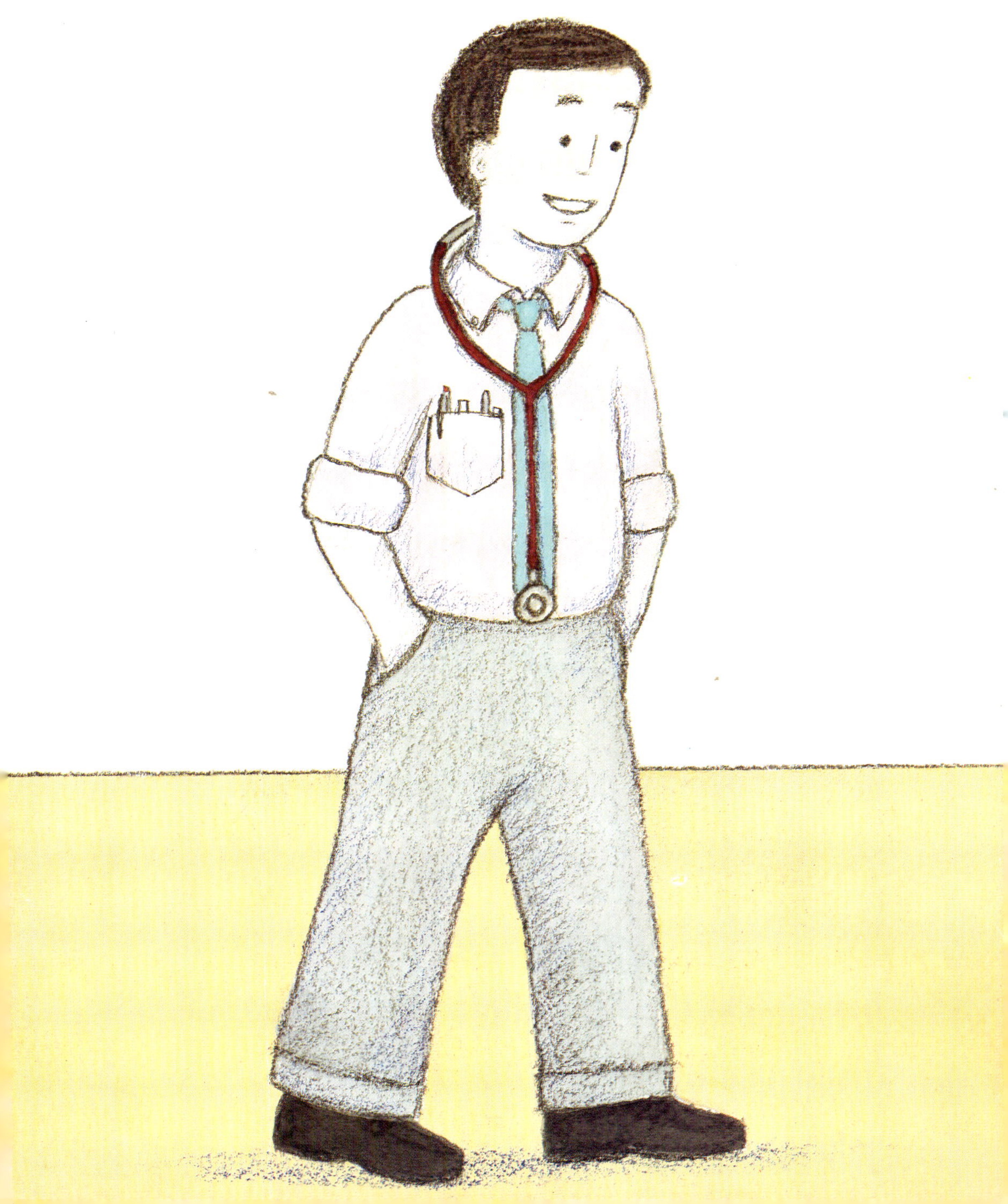

around Joey's arm.
then slowly lets the air out.

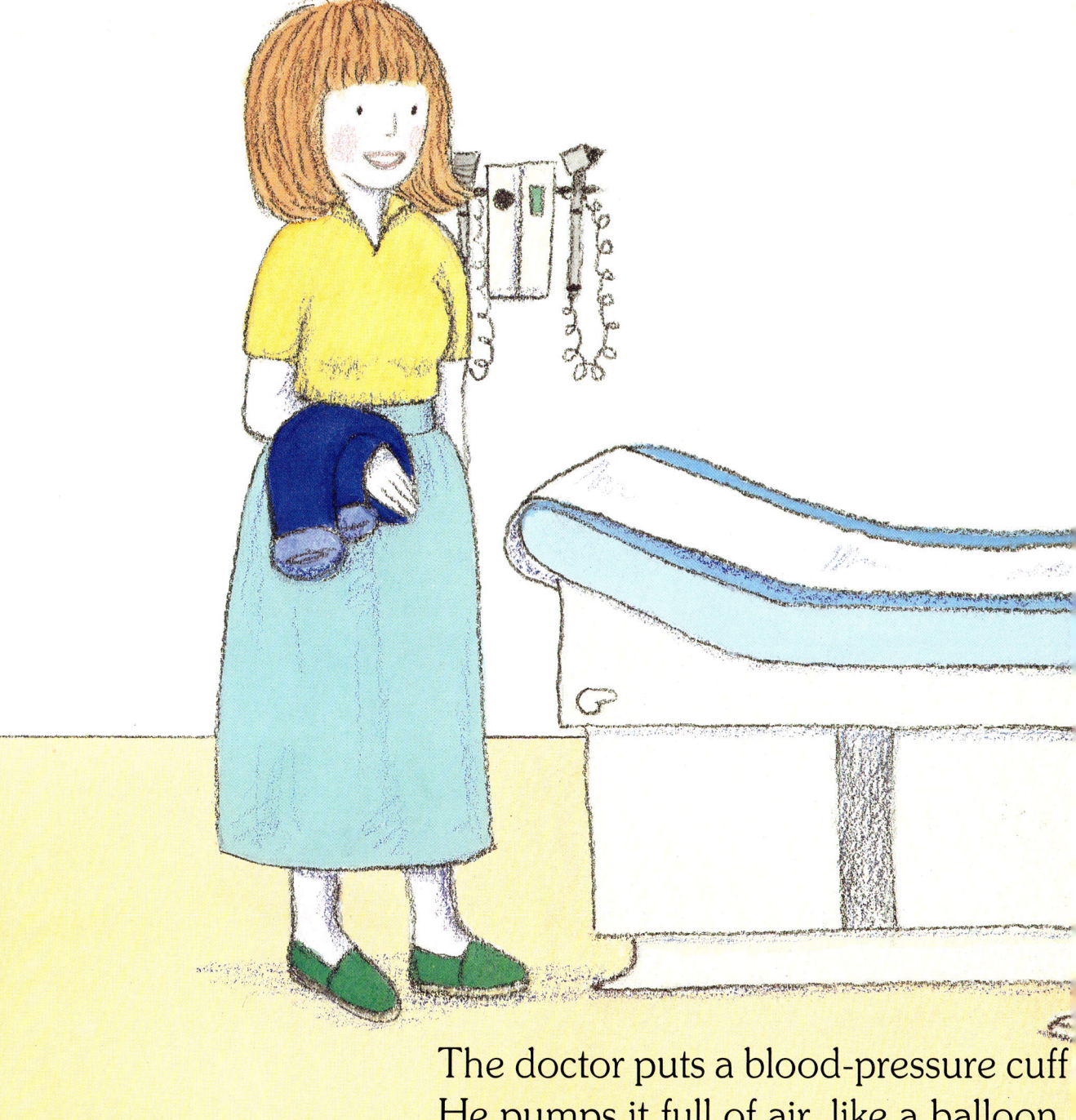

The doctor puts a blood-pressure cuff
He pumps it full of air, like a balloon,

Who is going to give Joey an injection?
The doctor.
What will the doctor use?
See if you can guess.

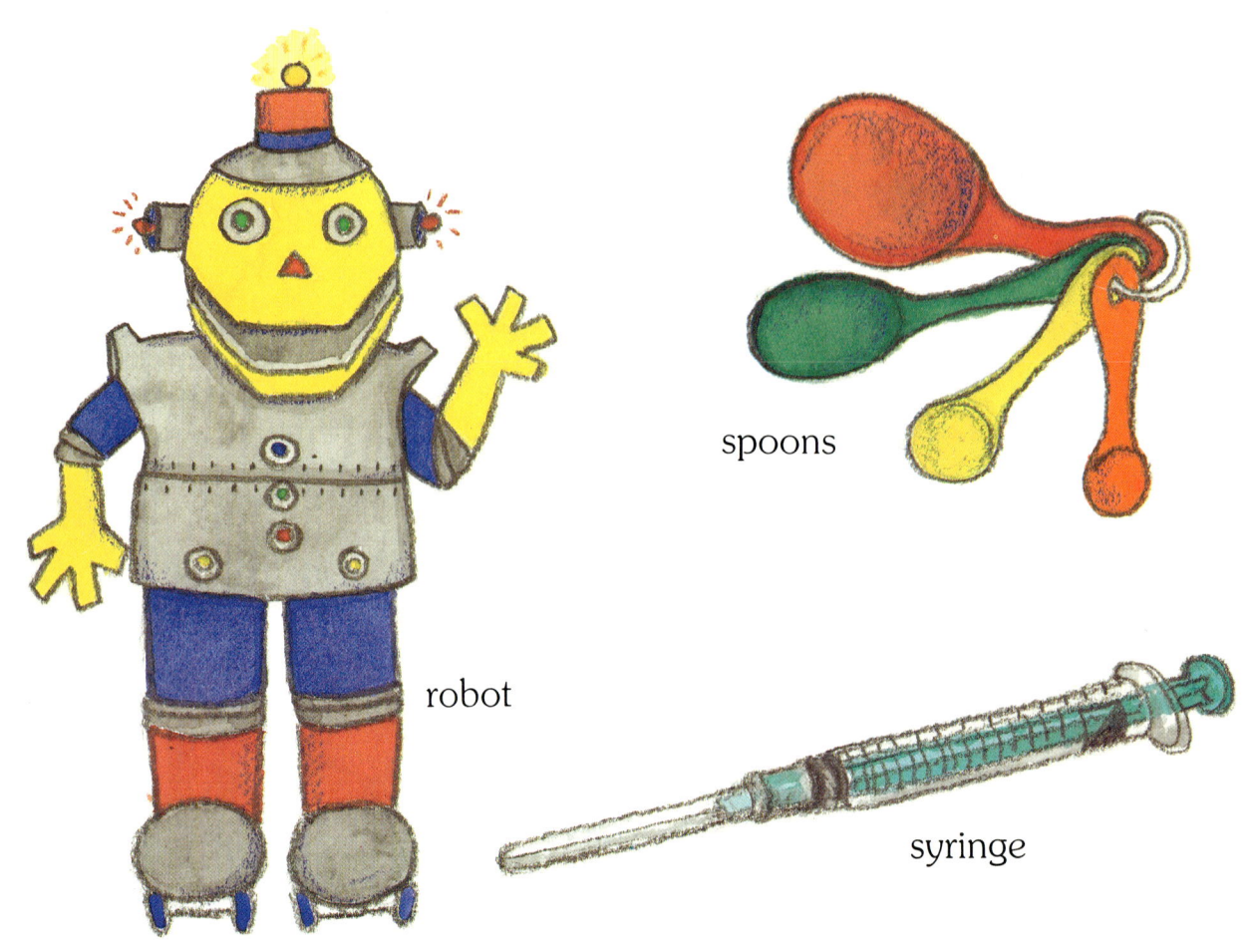

spoons

robot

syringe

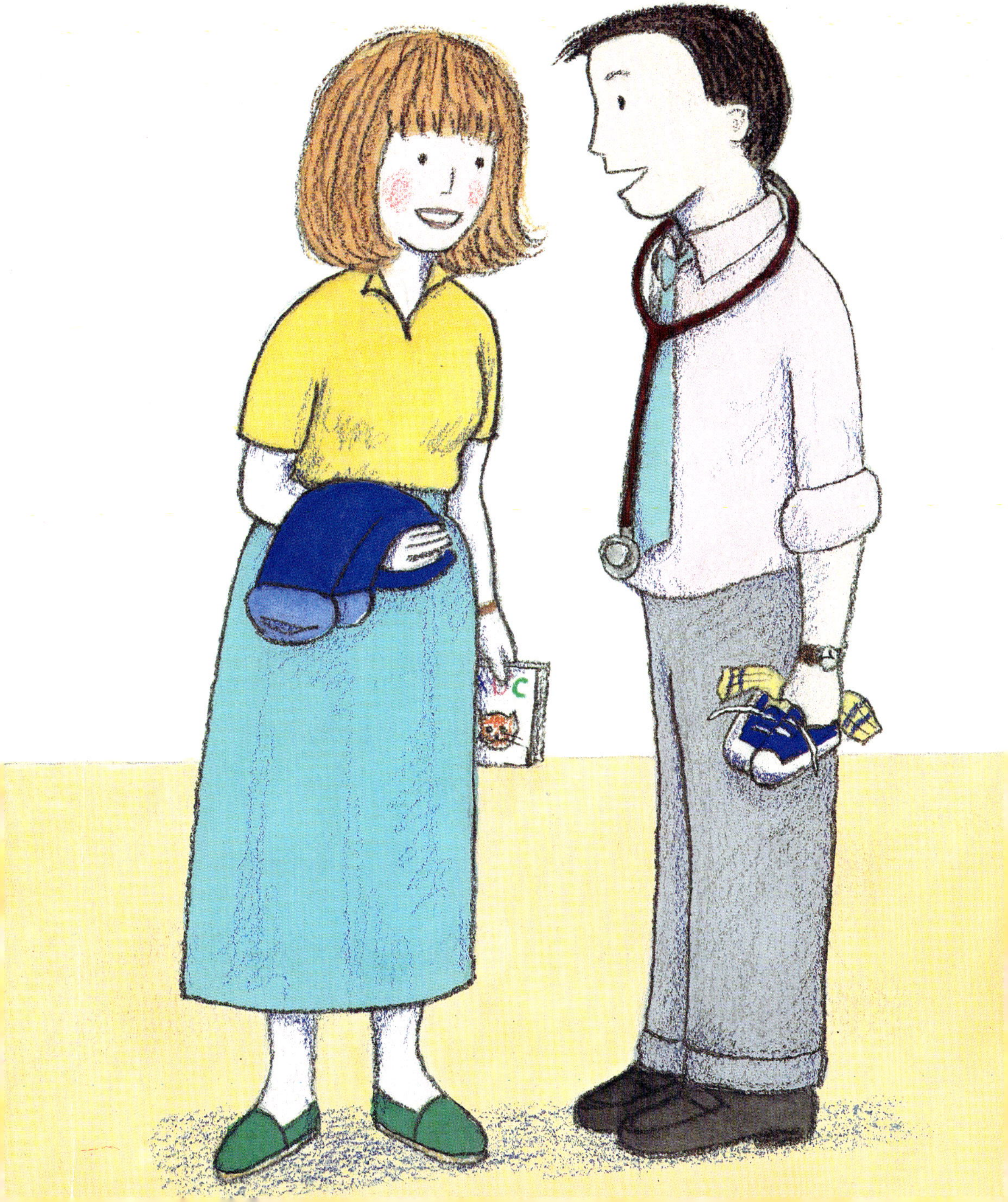

injects medicine to protect Joey from disease.

The needle hurts Joey's arm for a moment. The syringe

Good-bye, Joey!